WITH

LIGHT

By Eiji Orii and Masako Orii   Pictures by Kimimaro Yoshida

Gareth Stevens Children's Books
Milwaukee

Library of Congress Cataloging-in-Publication Data

Orii, Eiji, 1909-
    Simple science experiments with light / Eiji Orii and Masako Orii;
Kimimaro Yoshida, ill.
          p. cm. — (Simple science experiments)
    Includes index.
    Summary: Presents experiments, most of which use water, to demonstrate properties of shadow and light.
    ISBN 1-555-32858-X
    1. Light—Experiments—Juvenile literature. 2. Shades and
shadows—Experiments—Juvenile literature. [1. Shadows-
-Experiments. 2. Light—Experiments. 3. Experiments.] I. Orii,
Masako. II. Yoshida, Kimimaro, ill. III. Title. IV. Series.
QC360.075 1989
535'.07'8—dc19   88-23306

North American edition first published in 1989 by

Gareth Stevens Children's Books
7317 West Green Tree Road
Milwaukee, Wisconsin 53223, USA

This US edition copyright ©1989. First published as *Hikari No Itazura (Let's Try Light)* in Japan with an
original copyright © 1988 by Eiji Orii, Masako Orii, and Kimimaro Yoshida. English translation rights arranged
with Dainippon-Tosho Publishing Co., Ltd., through Japan Foreign-Rights Centre, Tokyo.

Additional text and illustrations copyright © 1989 by Gareth Stevens, Inc.

Series editor and additional text: Rita Reitci
Research editor: Scott Enk
Additional illustrations: John Stroh
Design: Laurie Shock
Translated from the Japanese by Jun Amano
Technical consultant: Jonathan Knopp, Chair, Science Department, Rufus King High School, Milwaukee

1 2 3 4 5 6 7 8 9 94 93 92 91 90 89

Light helps us to see. But it can also do other amazing
things. The straight lines of light can change direction, or
bend. Light can make things appear larger or smaller. Light
can shift images to different places. And light's
shadows can tell us things or entertain us.

This book will show you some easy ways to make light do
some surprising tricks!

A candle seems to be burning in water. Do you want to try making this happen? If you do, be sure you ask an adult to help you.

Put a glass of water on a table. Place a candle in front
of the glass and ask an adult to light it for you. The top
of the flame should be lower than the top of the water
in the glass.

Hold a small sheet of glass between the candle and the
water glass. Look through the glass sheet at the water
glass.   A candle seems to be burning in the water.

Get a candle the same size as the first one. Do not light the second candle. Take away the water glass and put the second candle in its place, right behind the first candle. What do you see this time?

The candle behind the glass sheet looks as if it, too, were lighted.

The shiny glass surface acts like a mirror that lets you look at things behind it. Look for reflections in the windows of your house.

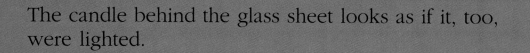

Catching a shadow can be easy — or hard.

If you're planning to play shadow tag and don't want to get caught, is it better to run toward the Sun or to run away from the Sun?

If you run toward the Sun, is your shadow easy to catch?

If you run away from the Sun, where is your shadow now?

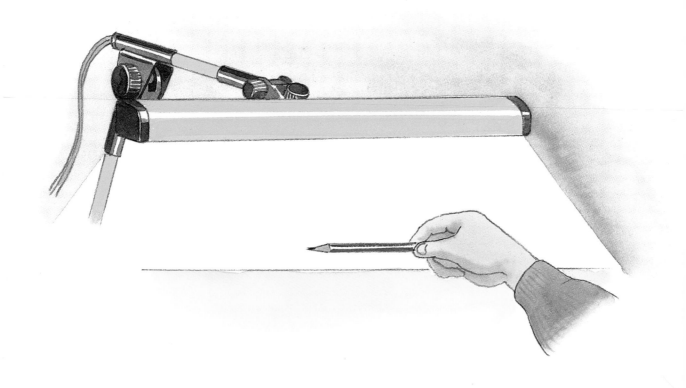

The fluorescent tubes lighting most factories and offices provide bright light with few dark shadows.

Hold a pencil or another object close up under a fluorescent light. Then lower the pencil close to the table below. What do you find out about the shadow?

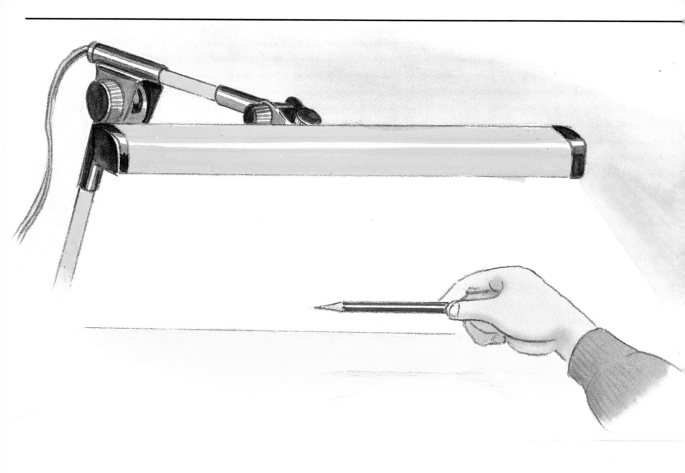

You do not see a dark shadow until you hold the pencil close to the table.

The darkest shadows are cast when light comes from a single point, like a light bulb. With fluorescent tubes, the light comes out all along the length of the tube. So these rays light objects on many sides. The only way to get a dark shadow with a fluorescent tube is to hold the object close enough to a surface to cut off most of the light rays.

Make your own shadow pictures.

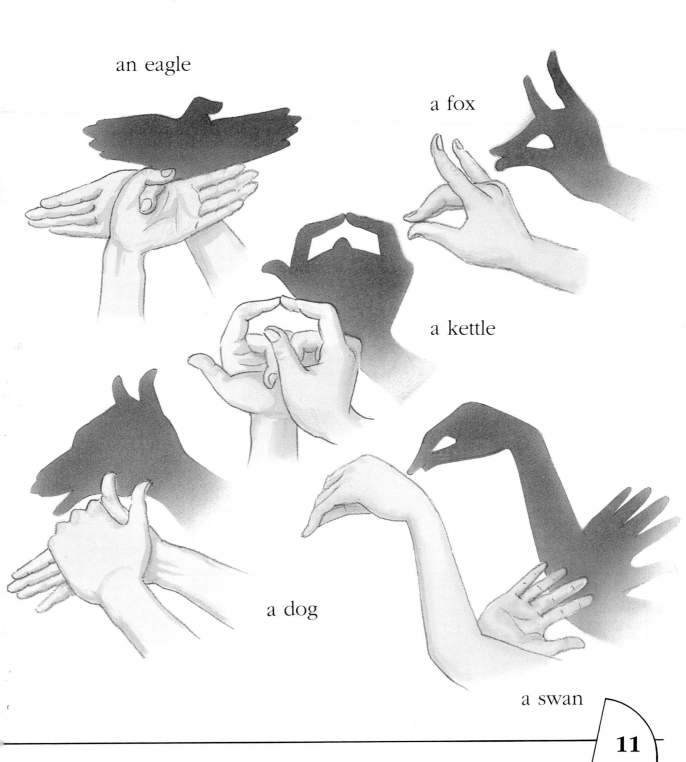

an eagle

a fox

a kettle

a dog

a swan

Light rays shine out straight in all directions from the source of the light. In a dark room, shine a flashlight at a comb and watch the shadow.

Move the flashlight away from the comb. Then move it up close. What happens?

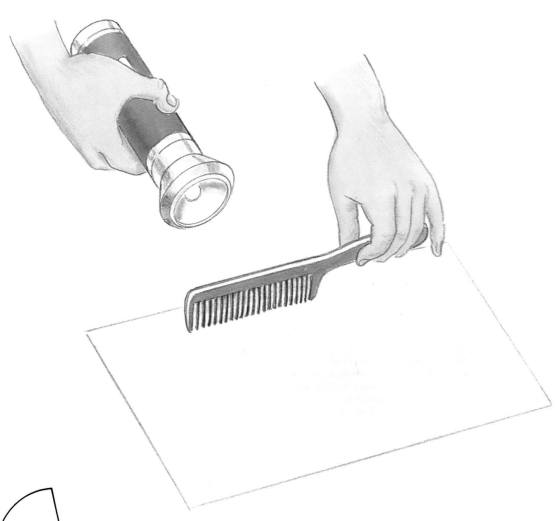

From farther away, only the light rays that shine straight ahead reach the comb.

With the flashlight closer to the comb, notice how the shadows fan out. This shows that light rays shine straight out on all sides from the source.

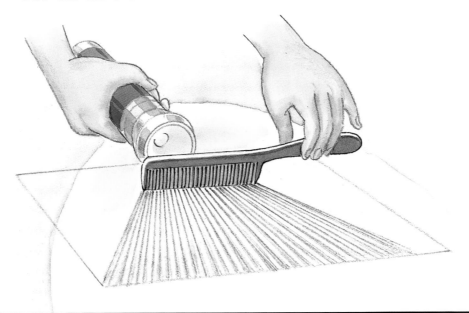

Now try this in sunlight. Near a sunny window, hold the comb straight up and down on paper. What kind of shadow does the Sun cast?

What happens when you slant the comb away from the Sun?

Shadows formed by the Sun's rays do not fan out. The rays strike the Earth straight on, or parallel, and cast shadows that we also say are parallel.

Even the longest shadows of the Sun, those at sunrise and sunset, are parallel.

Place a cup of water in the sunlight so that the rim of the cup casts its shadow on the water inside it. Now hold a stick straight up and down close to the water's surface.

What happens if you:

touch the water's surface with the stick?
put the stick deep in the water?
dip the stick in and out of the water?

A dent in the water surface casts a round shadow. A cup's curved surface brings light to a bright point on the water.

Stick dents water surface — dent's shadow is ball-shaped.

Stick is in the water — ball shadow stays at surface.

Stick dips in and out — shadow and light flash.

What kind of shadow does a spoon have?

Hold the spoon with the round side toward the light. Bring the spoon close to the surface of the water. Watch the spoon's shadow closely.

Touch the water surface with the spoon and then put it in the water.

Turn the spoon's bowl toward the light. What kind of shadow do you see now?

Try this with a fork.

Light shines through clear objects, throwing their colors onto the table. Light that cannot shine through objects makes their shadows dark.

While you are taking a bath, put your hand under the water and point your finger upward. Now turn your finger sideways under the water. Compare this with your finger held above the water.

The size of your finger seems to change as you change the position of your finger.

Water bends light rays, making things look bigger.

Place a cup on a table and put a coin inside it. Take 2 or 3 steps backward until you can no longer see the coin. Without moving, ask someone to pour water into the cup. What happens?

That's strange! Now you can see the coin.

The coin is not really where it seems to be. Water bends the light rays and forms the image of the coin above its real place. So the coin seems to be higher up.

Put a coin in an empty glass. Fill a big bowl with water. Now place the glass inside the bowl and look at the glass from the side. What do you see?

Where did the coin go?

When an empty glass is surrounded by water, it acts like a mirror. The reflection of the bowl on the sides of the glass hides the coin inside.

Now fill the glass with water.

Surprise! The coin is back.

The glass no longer acts like a mirror because it is full of water. Now you can see the coin inside it.

Cut a small drawing or cartoon from a newspaper. Tape the picture upside down inside a glass. Cover the glass with a rubber band around plastic wrap or a plastic bag so that water cannot get inside. Put the glass upside down in a bowl of water. What happens to the picture?

Next set the glass sideways in the bowl of water. What do you see now?

Why can't you see the picture inside the empty glass?
What do you see reflected on the glass?

The picture looks much smaller. The curved side of the glass makes light rays come together so that things seem to shrink.

Put a coin on a table. Place an empty glass on top of the coin and cover the glass with a saucer. Can you see the coin from the side?

Fill the glass nearly to the top with water and put the saucer back on. What happens?

Has the water bent the light so that the coin's image forms in another place?

A cat is stalking a mouse. Can you save the mouse?

Ask an adult to photocopy this page. Use the photocopy when you follow the directions below.

Place a glass of water on the mouse and cover the glass with a saucer.

GLOSSARY

Here is a list of words and phrases used in this book. After you read what each word or phrase means, you can see it used in a sentence.

angle: two straight lines going away from a point
The sidewalk left the building at an angle.

cast: to throw, to cause to fall, to give forth
The boy cast his fish line into the deep pond.

dent: a slight hollow made in a surface
His new car has a dent in it.

fluorescent tube: a glass tube coated on the inside with a chemical and filled with a gas that gives light when an electric current is turned on
He replaced the burned-out fluorescent tube.

image: a duplicate or reproduction or likeness of something
The photograph was a good image of his dog.

light rays: the smallest stream of light from any source
The light rays from the Sun are extremely strong.

parallel: two lines that are equal distances apart and never touch
The railroad tracks are parallel.

reflection: an image or likeness thrown back from a surface
He saw his reflection in the clean store window.

shadow: a dark image made by something that stands between a light source and a surface
They sat in the shadow of the tree.

shrink: to become smaller or to make smaller
Will this sweater shrink if I throw it in the wash?

source: the point or thing from which something starts out
The Sun is the source of all the Earth's energy.

stalking: following or sneaking up on
The wolf is stalking the deer.

surface: the outside layer of anything
The surface of the road is rough.

INDEX